Tundra—a huge, treeless plain bordering the Arctic Ocean. **Alpine tundras** are found on mountain slopes at altitudes where trees cannot grow.

Valley—a gently sloping depression between hills or mountains. A stream flows along the floor of many valleys. Small valleys with creeks flowing through them are called **hollows**.

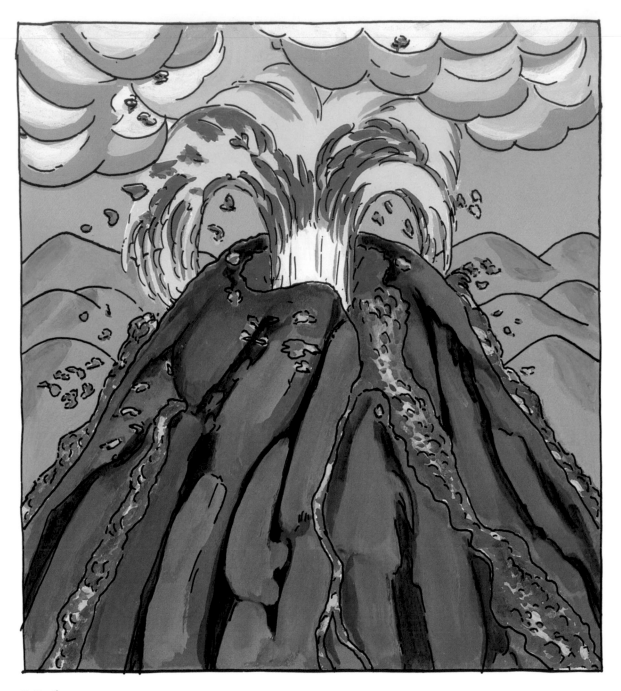

Volcano—an opening or vent in the earth's crust through which ashes, hot gases, and lava erupt. **Lava** is a fiery liquid formed of hot, melted rock. As lava cools, it often forms cone-shaped mountains.

Waterfall—a stream that flows over the edge of a cliff. There are two types of waterfalls.

Cataract—a large, dramatic waterfall that plunges down from a high, overhanging precipice.

Cascade—a small, splashing waterfall that tumbles down a mountainside in a series of steps.

cataract

cascade

Zone—a broad belt of climate and geography that encircles the earth. There are five zones on the earth.

Tropical or **torrid zone**—the hot, steamy region that lies just north and south of the equator.

Temperate zones—the two moderate regions that lie north of and south of the tropical zone. Each zone has hot summers, cold winters, and milder seasons in between.

Polar zones—the icy-cold regions at each pole. The northern polar zone, named the **Arctic**, is at the top of the earth. The southern zone, named the **Antarctic**, is at the bottom of the earth.

Index

Alpine tundra   43
Antarctic   46
Arctic   46

bank   42
berg   24
bitty berg   24
bluff   12
bog   28
brook   42

cascade   45
cataract   45
cavern   12
channel   41
chasm   11
coastline   10
continental slope   14
coral   8
cove   9
creek   42
crest   30

drainage basin   38

erosion   9
escarpment   34

floor   11

gap   31
geothermal   19
gorge   11
growler   24

gully   21
guyot   40

harbor   9
headland   36
hollow   43

inlet   9
isle   24
islet   24

knob   23
knoll   23

lagoon   8
lava   44
lowland   23

mesa   10
mount   30

narrows   41

oasis   16
ocean trench   33
oxbow lake   29

pampa   21
passage   41
peak   30
pinnacle   30,40
point   11
polar zones   46
pond   27

pool   27
prairie   21
precipice   12

quicksand   42

rain forest   26
ravine   11

sandbar   39
savanna   21
sea arch   40
sea stack   40
seashore   10
shoal   39
source   22
spit   11
spring   22
steppe   21
summit   30

tableland   35
temperate zones   46
torrent   21
torrid zone   46
tributary   38
tropical zone   46

veldt   21

watershed   38
wetland   28
white water   37
woodlands   18
woods   18